I MAY BE STUPID BUT
I'M NOT THAT STUPID

Selima Hill grew up in a family of painters on farms in England and Wales, and has lived by the sea in Dorset for over 35 years. She received a Cholmondeley Award in 1986, and was a Royal Literary Fund Fellow at Exeter University in 2003-06. She won first prize in the Arvon/*Observer* International Poetry Competition with part of *The Accumulation of Small Acts of Kindness* (1989), one of several extended sequences in *Gloria: Selected Poems* (Bloodaxe Books, 2008). *Gloria* includes work from *Saying Hello at the Station* (1984), *My Darling Camel* (1988), *A Little Book of Meat* (1993), *Aeroplanes of the World* (1994), *Violet* (1997), *Bunny* (2001), *Portrait of My Lover as a Horse* (2002), *Lou-Lou* (2004) and *Red Roses* (2006).

Her latest collections from Bloodaxe are: *The Hat* (2008); *Fruitcake* (2009); *People Who Like Meatballs* (2012), shortlisted for both the Forward Poetry Prize and the Costa Poetry Award; *The Sparkling Jewel of Naturism* (2014); *Jutland* (2015), shortlisted for both the T.S. Eliot Prize and the Roehampton Poetry Prize; *The Magnitude of My Sublime Existence* (2016), shortlisted for the Roehampton Poetry Prize; *Splash Like Jesus* (2017); and *I May Be Stupid But I'm Not That Stupid* (2019).

Violet was a Poetry Book Society Choice and was shortlisted for all three of the UK's major poetry prizes, the Forward Prize, T.S. Eliot Prize and Whitbread Poetry Award. *Bunny* won the Whitbread Poetry Award, was a Poetry Book Society Choice, and was shortlisted for the T.S. Eliot Prize. *Lou-Lou* and *The Hat* were Poetry Book Society Recommendations, while *Jutland* was a Special Commendation.

SELIMA HILL

I May Be Stupid But I'm Not That Stupid

BLOODAXE BOOKS

ISBN: 978 1 78037 191 7

First published 2019 by
Bloodaxe Books Ltd,
Eastburn,
South Park,
Hexham,
Northumberland NE46 1BS.

www.bloodaxebooks.com
For further information about Bloodaxe titles
please visit our website and join our mailing list
or write to the above address for a catalogue

Supported using public funding by
ARTS COUNCIL
ENGLAND

Cover design: Neil Astley & Pamela Robertson-Pearce.

Printed in Great Britain by Bell & Bain Limited, Glasgow, Scotland, on
acid-free paper sourced from mills with FSC chain of custody certification.

ACKNOWLEDGEMENTS

Fishtank was published as a pamphlet by Flarestack Poets in 2018 and was a PBS Autumn Pamphlet Choice. 'Heaven' (from *The Boxer Klitschko*) won the Poetry London Clore Prize 2018 third prize.

I would like to thank Penny Dunscombe for her patience: she is even more pedantic than I am.

I would also like to thank Jo Hawkins and Lorraine Knowles – long live librarians! – and Rachel Hawkes, literary archivist at Newcastle University, and, finally, Alexander Bearman-Kossykh (and not only because I like his name and his dog's name).

CONTENTS

Elective Mute

My Mother and Me on the Eve of the Chess Championships

Lambchop

The Boxer Klitschko

Helpless with Laughter

ELECTIVE MUTE

The Fire

My cot caught fire but I didn't cry
so something wasn't right from the beginning

and nobody must think they are to blame
for how I was and everything that happened.

Thousands upon Thousands of Beetles

I'm lying on my bed in my bandages
listening to the sounds far below me

of thousands upon thousands of beetles,
returning home from parties, being crushed.

Elastic

I squeeze and squeeze and squeeze and never stop
until the other person wriggles free

by telling God He's making a mistake
and could He please remake me from elastic.

The Bear

I love the bear because it is inert;
I love the way it stares straight ahead;

the way its navy velvet is so dry
it feels as if its forebears should be emery boards.

It Seems a Shame to Scream as Loud as Possible

It seems a shame to scream as loud as possible
because it makes them think there's something wrong

when actually it's me being me
and being me to me is hilarious.

I'm Sorry But I Think I Might Be Real

I'm sorry but I think I might be real.
If I think I'm not then I must be

and if I think I am I must be too.
Or am I being tricked in some way?

Am I being dreamt by a dreamer
who can't, or won't, console, or even contact me?

A dreamer who is bigger than the universe
into which she squeezes like marshmallow.

Summer Days

The summer days are flying by like angels
but I can make no sense of them at all

and spend the day lying in the river
where sense is no more use to me than pickle.

There's More to Life Than Swimming

Never let the doctors try and tell you
there's more to life than swimming when there's not –

swimming is my way of being special
when special isn't special but afloat.

Death and the Smell of Almonds

I can hardly breathe, far less think,
my little heart is going *thump, thump, thump,*

my teacher's going *very well, don't smell them then,*
but if I don't I'll die. OK, I'll die.

Coconut

I used to be a woman who could talk
but now am mute. I didn't choose to be

any more than, say, a normal mariner
chooses to be washed up on an island

so remote from any other island
the only thing to do is do nothing

and years go by and when at last they come
nobody recognises him,

he doesn't even recognise himself,
his hair is coarse and he speaks not.

Dumb

I never know I'm not saying anything.
I think I just assume I know I can

if and when it ever seems necessary.
Fire alarms are dumb like I am too.

The Wedding-cake

Being me is fun. To other people
the me that I *parade around* in front of them,

tossing my big head like a caber
that wants to be a wedding-cake, is not.

PLEASE CARRY DOGS

When I see the sign I turn back
because I haven't got a dog to carry.

Cows in Dreams

Cows in dreams who tolerate everything,
even me, the child who has fun

at everybody else's expense,
are more like my own mother than my mother.

Rubber Bands

Rubber bands, drill bits and tomatoes
and people turning somersaults and jazz

being played in rooms I can't escape from
and gravel drives make me feel nervous.

DEPTH CHANGE

Marvelling at the five concurrent consonants,
I fall into the deep end by mistake

but how can I explain to the lifeguard
the letters that I'm reading make no sense?

Them

If I wasn't me, I would be them.
If I wasn't me, and *lost for words*,

I would know exactly what to say
and what the point of saying it would be.

My Mother

Everyone is strange, but, alas,
my mother is the strangest of them all.

She seems to be so disappointed in me.
Also it's as if she is afraid of me.

My Head

My head is like a sack full of sacks.
There's nobody to play with but me.

Banging my big head will get me nowhere
but banging it is making perfect sense.

Chatty

Long ago I used to be quite chatty.
I'd chat away and never even look

down the long red drives that lead to hospitals
where people who are not chatty live.

Made Entirely of Roses

If a cow were made entirely of roses,
producing only rose milk, her rose calves

would be like aphids – green, in other words,
and much too simple-minded to be frightening.

Tiddlywinks

Why aren't people good? And why o why
has everyone got faces like the tiddlywinks

my father likes to entertain his friends with
by sending me to find them in the flower-beds?

My Darling Spiders

Don't ask me why I spend the whole weekend
sitting in the silence of the airing-cupboard

with spiders walking up and down my arm
but anyway I do and we like it.

Football

Seeing what the coach calls *the football team*
thundering towards me in the mud,

I'm trying to explain I'm a person
who doesn't even know what football is;

who's not so much a person as a sheep
who doesn't even know what a daisy is.

My First Boyfriend

The thought of being someone someone sees
makes me feel very uneasy

and therefore this new person is ideal
because he is *as blind as a bat!*

If It Gets Too Noisy

If it gets too noisy I pass out
and people find me lying on the floor

with nothing else to do but be a floorboard
and celebrate the absence of my ears.

My Wettened Balaclava

All I want to do is find a basin
and stand there with my head underwater

until I feel better or at least
let me wear my wettened balaclava.

My Second Boyfriend

People say I'm rude and I *am* rude.
I know I am. But I wish I wasn't.

For instance, when he takes me to the sea,
I run across the sand and just keep going,

my filthy dress billowing around me,
leaving him to drive home alone.

Blue Murder

Being touched feels like I'm sizzling.
I feel like a chip dropped in oil.

I used to shut my eyes and scream blue murder.
Now I know not to do that.

Rubies

If a cow were made entirely of rubies
her ruby calf would never cause her pain

but all day long they would stand apart
gazing at each other indifferently.

Snouts

Because I find it hard decoding faces,
I recognise the doctors by their shoes:

I see the shiny shoes as pairs of snouts
peeping out like the snouts of weasels.

Comfort

To other people, people are a comfort.
To me they are a threat: they lift me up

and lock me in a side-room like a trout
to watch the seething of the slippery motes.

Sweetcorn

I mustn't swing the sweetcorn by its hair;
I mustn't feel sick or start skipping;

I mustn't think I mustn't step on mats;
I mustn't sniff the chair; and when they say

'Tea or coffee?' *I must answer them*
and if that's hard it's not allowed to be.

Cocoa

This is what it's like to be me.
Sometimes people slap me or kick me.

I don't mind. I'm a slick of cocoa powder.
Cocoa doesn't speak or even see.

Fear

Fitting things together – closing gates
or putting on socks, for example,

or laying a viola in its case,
a baby in your lap – allays fear.

The Catastrophic Driving Lesson

The traffic looks like nothing else but angles.
However much they shout at me, I'm stuck.

It seems to be the same with people's faces:
I cannot seem to see what I'm seeing.

Watches

I have to ('have to'?) wear the same clothes
and, if I don't, I don't feel safe

and people's voices start to sound like chalk
and people's faces shrink and jerk like watches.

Other People

Other people can and do drive cars,
eat zabaglione and have sex

and recognise each other in the park,
even in their extraterrestrial bobble-hats.

Rubber Cow

If a cow were made entirely of rubber,
her daughter would be made of rubber too,

whose rubber brain would be incapable
of doing what my mother's daughter's does.

Purple Eel-grass

My brain is like a brain made of eel-grass
swaying in a car made of pond

but look – I look so normal I look normal,
I look like someone who can drive with ease.

To Disentangle Wool

If praying is to practice (which it is)
feeling what it's like to feel like me

being not just me but being *everyone*,
to disentangle wool is like praying.

Happiness

Even now, although I know it's wrong,
when I feel happy I'm so happy

I find myself exploding into signing
or what they call *lapsing into sign*.

How to Smile

The trouble is I don't say a word
or else I say too much, which is worse,

but either way, however hard I try,
I cannot seem to work out how to smile properly.

Telephone Numbers

First I hear the words from someone's voice
then I say the words in my head

then I have to see the sounds I hear
and then I have to make them leave my head

and, as they leave, I have to change their colour
to match them up with figures on the keypad

and finally I must locate the hand
on which I am to activate the index finger.

Convivial

Convivial is my favourite word
because it's got two v's and the v's

override the fact that what it means
is something I can no more love than varices.

The Slowness of the Slow

The slowness of the very slow – like tar,
elephants, the alternating tides,

trains in autumn, bored telephonists,
men in dresses drifting through Japan –

the slowness of the slow feels right.
Box is another example.

Electricity

I force myself to touch electric fences
every day, or every other day,

in just the same humiliating way
my mother must have struggled to touch me.

You and Me

I can't see how the person you are talking to
can be the one I'm thinking of as me

who can't imagine what it must be like
to be the you you're thinking of as you.

Coffee

When someone comes and offers me some coffee
I sometimes don't reply: I don't reply

because my brain's already somewhere else
and can't remember what the person's question was.

Queen

Although I know it's not the one I'm waiting for,
although it's going somewhere else entirely,

I step inside it like a lost queen
who doesn't even know what trains are for.

Conversation in a Sheep Field

It's hard to both see the sheep as sheep
and carry on talking, for example;

and being touched while I'm trying to listen
can stop the words I'm listening to make sense.

Having Fun

When I'm being me, I'm having fun –
or should that be *I used to have fun*

before I fell apart so spectacularly
and had to start again from the beginning?

Seventeen Sheep

My counting sheep makes them last for ever.
Not only sheep. I make the sun, the gate,

the beetle underfoot, last for ever.
I make the future bow to my command.

Children and Adults

I've always got on better with children
except when I myself was a child

and then I got on better with adults,
among whose number I am now counted.

Rothko and Mints

To suck a mint while studying the Rothko
seems to make my studying complete

just as, in the silence of the hospital,
to count the pips completed my pain.

My Third Boyfriend's Sunbed

Sunbeds, like depilatories and power-tools,
pretend they're there to help you but they're not

and nothing will induce me to approach one.
Poodle-skirts and decimals, the same.

Tickles

I went into the hat shop with a friend
but had to leave because it was too tickly,

so much so I found it hard to speak
and, when I did, all I said was *Speak to me.*

Praise and Dust

Being praised – by anyone, for anything –
bewilders me, frightens me even,

and people's faces, like unanswered questions
in empty corridors, return to dust.

Arson

Arson, rain, a ton, my tulips, fur,
cattle, beetroot, lists, the letter v –

if God had only given them some hands
these hands would be the hands I would be searching for.

OK, OK, OK

I wish it was OK to be belittled
because I sometimes like to feel little;

I wish it was OK to ask a stranger
to squeeze my chest so tight I can't breathe.

Aphid

I'd rather be a cow than a woman
and I'd rather be an aphid than a cow –

an aphid-coloured aphid with a brain
that tells it what to do and it does it.

Hazelnuts

I'm balancing an onion on my eiderdown
to force myself to cook myself a meal

while thinking to myself it would be simpler
if God agreed to let me live on hazelnuts.

The Woman in the Changing-room and Me

The woman without glasses in the changing-room
says she doesn't know who I am

and do I tell her? No: I assume
I myself therefore don't know either.

She Follows Me Around and Upsets Me

She follows me around and upsets me,
and not just me, she upsets everyone,

but nobody can get her to go home,
if, that is, she's even got a home;

I mean, she seems to think she lives with me,
it's like I'm me but also someone else –

this other person, who I've never met,
and hasn't even got her own body.

In Love with Roger Federer

I know it isn't clever to be clever
and not to drive and not to drink coffee

and not to be in love with Roger Federer
and I should be ashamed – and I am.

Swallow

The trouble is when you talk to me
and when I'm making sense of what you're saying

it's hard to swallow at the same time.
(By swallow I mean swallow and not swallow.)

Black and White Buttons

Do I press the black one or the white one?
'Either,' says the doctor; but the nurse,

although she knows 'either' is correct,
answers 'white' to simplify it for me.

Why I Like Fish

I think I might have never been in love
– except with fish: I find it hard to talk

and, with fish, you don't have to talk
and that's why I like fish: they don't talk.

People Who Wear Bobble-hats

Cleanliness is next to who or what
and who has special needs and who has not
and what's the point of being normal anyhow
and all that glitters is not what and why
and asking normal people normal questions
will get you nowhere as we all know
and bobble-hats like that will get you nowhere
especially when you wear them when you're hot.

The Huggers

When people say they like to *paint the flowers*,
they don't mean paint the flowers but paint the canvas;

when they say they're sleeping *on the train*,
they don't mean on, they mean inside, the train;

and when they say *can I have a hug*
and walk towards you holding out their arms,

what they really mean, I know this now,
is *Even if you say I can't I'm going to.*

Camping

I get the torch but when it doesn't work
I stumble through the darkness with my eyes closed!

Grab a Wrap

I think they think I think I'm so *clever*
when all I want to be is be like them:

have a shower, make a quick phone call,
grab a wrap, think nothing of it.

Simple Dunes

My head is like a head full of eggs
laid by larks in hollows in the dunes

which, after lying modestly like sand,
suddenly make for the sky.

Skin

I wish there wasn't such a thing as skin,
or such a thing as food, or as love –

or such a thing as what they call love,
that wavers, and that thus insults love's name.

Havoc and Graciousness

After sixty years of causing havoc
I've finally decided to be gracious

just as all my sixty-year-old colleagues
have finally decided not to bother.

Kangaroo

When even my best friend wants to strangle me
I must be doing something wrong – and, sadly,

one fine day, she does want to strangle me:
it's when I start jumping up and down.

How to Sparkle

When I feel afraid, I line things up,
like lining up these words, for example;

but why do people seem afraid of *me*?
And how do people know how to sparkle?

A Bird on a Cow

My brain is like a bird on a cow
that's singing in her ear about a universe

where gravel drives have yet to be invented
and birds and beetles answer to their names.

Empathy, Empathy, Empathy

Empathy, empathy, empathy!
They always say I lack it about *them*

but, to me, they lack it about *me*,
although, of course, they're better at expressing it –

expressing it or not expressing it;
at saying this but knowing they mean that.

Potato

They think that I must want to be different
when actually I want to be the same.

I feel like a boiled potato
with a boiled beetle inside it.

I'm not just being rude. I'm all wrong.
I don't know who we are. I'm exhausted.

Octopuses

How come other people wear mascara
and how come other people are so kind

and why are PG Tips called PG Tips
and anyhow who cares and one last thing –

can I call the octopuses octopi
and if I can my joy will know no bounds.

A Person with a Saw and Some Chocolates

When I'm dead a person with a saw
can saw my head in half and make two bowls

to pour, or shake, a box of chocolates into
and then the person with the saw can eat them.

MY MOTHER AND ME ON THE EVE
OF THE CHESS CHAMPIONSHIPS

My Mother's Underwear

My mother's giant salmon-pink underwear
is pressed against the bars of my cot

exuding, in the light of passing cars,
my mother's sickly smell of warm rubber.

My Mother on a Rock with a Sketchbook

She carries her inflatable cushion
across the windswept beach to the rock

on which she sits, today as every day,
to draw my back, my buckets and my castles.

The Precious Moments of My Mother's Life

The precious moments of my mother's life –
and they are, or will be, very precious –

are bobbing out of sight in their thousands
like plastic bottles bobbing out to sea.

My Mother's Handkerchiefs

My mother has a hundred boiled handkerchiefs
she keeps beside her bed in a drawer

in which at night I hear them re-arrange themselves
like girls who have been brainwashed to be cruel.

My Mother's Jeans

They're pale blue, with paler blue turn-ups,
and pulled in at the waist with a belt –

like a little five-year-old cowgirl's!
I'm ashamed to even have to look at them.

Please can she be taken back upstairs
and dressed in an appropriate skirt.

My Mother's Powder

When my mother powders her nose
it makes me feel dizzy, for some reason,

as if the smell of powder was a ʒ
or, bolder still, a ʤ as in ju*dg*e.

My Mother in the Shoe Shop

She creeps, she cries, she coughs but rarely talks,
about the shoes or anything else.

Another thing, she never comes to school,
she never sees me in my uniform,

she never sees the room in which I dream,
fast asleep in my new shoes.

My Mother in Her Nightdress

What feel like the wings of legless insects
trapped inside my baby-blue dressing-gown

is nothing but my mother in her nightdress
brushing past me unexpectedly.

My Mother in the Drawing-room

My mother's planting *choux* in the drawing-room.
I can't believe my eyes but it's true.

She's rolling up her sleeves like young Kamchatka girls.
I've never seen my mother look so happy!

My Mother in August

In order to protect me from the women
sweating on the poolside like onions,

who only use the water to wee in,
she'll only let me swim in the sea.

My Mother's Petticoat

She slips between the sheets in her petticoat,
still holding in her hand the large handkerchief

she never goes anywhere without,
and cries herself to sleep until tea-time.

My Mother in the Studio

Of course the sickly smell of warm rubber,
the sight of snail-drowners drowning snails,

of little boys on quiet country lanes
in cardboard boxes waiting for the cars,

of stuffed giraffes, the melancholy sound
of someone drumming in a smoky room

make me feel sick but not as sick
as witnessing her fear of cats and kittens.

My Mother's Omelettes

Although my mother only eats omelettes,
she feeds her husband oranges and meat

which doesn't seem to help with the temper
that towers above us like apartment blocks.

My Mother and Me in the Library

This is where the men we mustn't see
hide themselves away, or think they do,

behind the papers, in between the stacks,
but my mother knows where they are.

My Mother in a Swimsuit

She's standing in the sea in a swimsuit
trying to look as if she's fully dressed

but whose it was, or is, remains a mystery
I'm much too young and innocent to fathom.

My Mother's Husband

My mother tries to keep the house in order –
just as she imagines God Himself

keeping things in order – but my mother,
unlike God, only makes things worse

and now her husband steps into a taxi
as if he's off to found a new world order.

My Mother's New Clogs

Dwarfed by the enormous wooden clogs
whose gladioli colours she ignores,

she's standing in the mud on shredded cabbage-stalks
being pecked by seven pea-brained chickens.

My Mother on a Mountain-top

Every day she makes us Apple Snow
and every day she says *it's not quite right*

like someone on a mountain-top inventing
more and more ways to be perfect.

My Mother on Holiday

The most important thing about a castle's
assessing the consistency of sands.

If she thinks I must be getting hungry,
nothing could be further from the truth.

She's welcome to her bread-and-butter sandwiches.
All I want's to hear the sand's *slaboshpytskiy*.

My Mother's Mother

She knows the hens that mooch about the kitchen
would never let the ghost of her mother –

if there *is* a ghost – so much as wave to her
(even though her mother got here first).

My Mother Keeps Bees

Forced to stay indoors, I see my mother
cross the yellow lawn in a boiler-suit!

It's white and dusty-looking, like the dustsheets
removal men might use for chandeliers.

My Mother's Hat

If you look closely, you can see her –
or, if not her, the ripples from her boat –

rowing off in search of adventure,
such as seeing rats, or a cow,

before returning to the river-bank
to nibble flapjacks in her floppy hat.

My Mother's Hair

My mother's hair is almost translucent
and looks as if it's only just been combed

although I've never even seen it loose.
I wish I liked it, like I do crests.

My Mother and the Great Dane

My mother, who denied me a penknife,
a pair of little studs or even sleepers,

or outings with the Chess Club to Torquay,
now turns away the motherless Great Dane.

My Mother with Flour on Her Hands

Each grain of flour, like a tiny fingernail,
is picking at the surface of my skin

as if I have offended it, but how?
And who am I supposed to say I'm sorry to?

My Mother and the Snails

No wonder she prefers the world of lettuces:
lettuces are never bored or cross;

and picking off the snails is quite restful,
then watching them meandering away.

My Mother's Book

It stays beside her bed, in her bedroom,
as if to keep at bay with all its listings

the fear she would deny of losing everything.
(She calls the book a book but it's a booklet.)

My Mother's Shoes

My mother's in the kitchen kneading dough
and no one is allowed to go in.

She makes the honey too, or, rather, gathers it,
and shiny honey drips and wriggles everywhere

like eels in the eel-pens of Japan.
Even her espadrilles are sticky.

My Mother's Washing

The petticoats of oyster-coloured silk
dripping in the mist on the washing-line

are whispering *she's here*, or hereabouts,
like scattered redshanks' legs whisper *peregrines*.

My Mother at the Tennis Courts

The man in tiny shorts is a doctor.
He stands beside my mother in his cardigan

and talks to her in that special way
doctors talk, who know that death is final.

My Mother Like a Bird

Every day she chirrups like a bird.
Every day I jingle like her chain.

My Mother at the House in Gortahork

The house is big and spooky, on a lake
I'm always being told not to swim in

and, when I do, the water, that looks black,
makes my naked body look like stars.

And once I met a man with a dog
and prayed to God not to tell my mother.

My Mother Plays Strip-Jack-Naked

The way my mother's playing Strip-Jack-Naked –
but why keep saying *playing*, it's pretending,

or drifting off, not even pretending,
and slowing me right down – is unbearable,

or should I say *almost* unbearable.
Part of me still knows I must be kind.

My Mother in Hangzhou

My mother has exhausted herself.
She's sobbed so hard she thought she'd never stop

and now she has exhausted herself
and never wants to sob like that again –

blub, sob, whatever you want to call it.
The tears behind her face are frozen solid.

Whatever it is she wants is unattainable,
whatever it is she thinks she's yearning for –

completeness, or completion, heaven knows –
whatever it is is simply unattainable.

And now she is exhausted, like the maids
battling with cocaine-encrusted toilet-pans

in Singapore, Los Angeles, Hangzhou,
exhausted maids who are afraid of everything.

My Mother and Small Children

My mother disapproves of small children,
anyone who's ill and lazy wives

but, most of all, she disapproves of me,
the way I look as bored as a hairdresser.

My Mother and Australia

Purity of heart. It sounds so beautiful.
She doesn't know exactly what it is

but still she knows she wants it, like Australia
is wanted by a small chained bird.

My Mother, Normally Such a Sweet Person

The very word – the fact that they exist,
the possibility of meeting one one day;

of me, her child, possibly becoming one;
of she, herself *(never to be mentioned)*

of she, herself, being, having been, one –
the very word horrifies my mother,

who, normally such a sweet person,
stiffens at the sound: *divorcee.*

My Mother in the Kitchen

My mother is alone in the kitchen
battling with this evening's Apple Snow

while upstairs in the bathroom I defy her
by taking off my nightdress *near the window*.

My Mother's Mortal Panic

My mother is as white as a sheet
but I maintain a haughty indifference

to what I think of as her *mortal panic*,
exacerbated by the smell of Cyclax.

My Mother by the Side of the Road

It's as if she's crying out for something
I was born to be dismissive of;

as if I'm at the wheel of a juggernaut
from whose great height I choose to see nothing.

My Mother's Ankles

I like to cultivate certain qualities.
Disinterestedness, for example.

My mother likes to cultivate *self-discipline*,
as those who've seen her exercise can testify.

My Mother's Sponge

I think my mother's frightened of me sometimes:
I'm up all night; I've got no friends; I scowl.

The closest I can get to feeling love towards her
is in the bath, alone with her sponge.

This Is How I Write About My Mother

This is how I write about my mother –
but something keeps on holding me back,

something I can't name, except to say
it feels like what feels like the opposite

of what I'm meaning by my own words;
it feels like I'm losing my nerve.

My Mother and the Oceans

All day long and far into the night
I swim until I'm swimming out of sight

across the coloured oceans of my brain.
Don't ask me why. It's not because I'm shy.

But mothers are too soft and I don't like them:
I don't like food and being crammed with food,

I don't like being touched, or even looked at,
I don't like being looked at like I'm someone

who all I ever do is only worry people,
I don't like high-pitched noises – so I swim.

My Mother's Car

As the years go by I get the feeling
it's hard for her, if not impossible,

not to give a name to the car
she likes to sit for hours in doing nothing.

Doing nothing? No, she is dreaming,
praying even, in her oily gloves.

My Mother's Purse

The things my mother keeps in her purse
must never be revealed. They are there

because it would be wrong to even think about them;
because it would unsettle what is settled.

She snatches it and shuts it with a click,
a click of desolation and foreboding.

My Mother and Flamingos

Never turn your nose up at flamingos,
never think you're here to be my friend,

never doubt my claim that mathematics
has other truths than being merely true,

and never fear kittens: only Kafka
can be allowed his painful fear of kittens.

My Mother's Silverware

Certain things she couldn't live without –
silver hallmarks, shoe-horns, gravel drives –

but other things she could: for example,
imagine if she lived without me,

irritating her all the time
like eel-blood the all-seeing eye-ball.

My Mother Plays Charades

The children watch wide-eyed from the sofa
as grandmama (who normally sits quietly,

unimpressed, the picture of misery)
is suddenly stamping her black feet.

My Mother Among the Butterflies

She picks her way through toys like fallen willows
where Speckled Woods still flit from leaf to leaf –

my fearless mother, who knows Right from Wrong;
who Time, however, shows no mercy to.

My Mother and the Sound of Chartreuse

Maybe I do love her after all,
maybe I don't know it but I do,

maybe I don't know what Love is
and maybe this is it, this creepy feeling,

this feeling that I dread, like being brushed against,
like shifting, with a *sh*, as in *Basia*,

pistachio, deliciousness, Chartreuse;
maybe I've just got to get used to it.

My Mother in the Car Park

Certain rules she knows she must obey:
she's not allowed to hug me or handle me

or dab me with her salmon-pink sponge;
she's not allowed to question or deny me;

she's not allowed to think I can't be trusted
when can't she see I know I think I can.

My Mother's Gloominess

She's ladylike but gloomy; for example,
she only ever likes to serve underarm.

She's also rather nervous. (We don't tell her
the tennis-balls were once the skulls of cats!)

The fact is – and I know she can't help it –
it doesn't suit her, being my mother.

My Mother and the Rabbit

She, my mother, is, to a mother,
as a Belgian Hare is to a hare;

elusive as salukis or gazelles
made of silver slyly turning gold,

born to be dissolved, or to dissolve,
like unattended horses in fine mist

that seem to float, that I would need to grow
another pair of ears to hear repeating

that every girl must be a grown woman
and every woman an obedient wife.

My Mother Like a Dress Made of Pins

What must it be like to be my mother?
My mother like a dress made of pins,

whose child doesn't know it's got a name
or even which way up it's meant to be

and thinks it's not a child but a fish
that doesn't need a mother but a lake

in which to live alone like a planet
endlessly encircling the deep.

My Mother at the Open-air Swimming-Pool

The towel is as scratchy as a cockroach.
(It's Finnish – it's supposed to be scratchy.)

An hour on dry land with my mother
proves to be as much as I can stand.

She walks about on tiptoe like the ostrich
across the arid regions of Namibia

and, like the ostrich, lacks stamina:
she looks as if she'd rather be a duster.

The swimming-pool attendant is watching us,
disarmingly matter-of-fact.

My Mother and the History of Art

My mother has been reading *Stones of Venice*
for forty years and never finished it.

In the car, on shopping trips, at picnics,
she carries it about like *Good News*.

Somebody, her husband perhaps,
has had it bound in pale green silk –

a book she'll never, in a million years,
admit to him to being bored to tears by.

My Mother's Mattress

Upstairs, in the heat, beside the handkerchiefs,
my mother's navy-blue horsehair mattress

still, although it's August, smells of damp,
of horses in the hush of damp forests,

of Spassky, still a child, playing chess
all day long, with nobody, in silence –

Spassky, whose seductive ingenuity
my mother has no need to understand.

My Mother and the Sea

She never reads the books the doctor brings.
In fact she'd like to chuck them in the sea

along with all the bills and all the catalogues
selling things like pantihose and cuckoo clocks.

My Mother and Me on the Eve
of the Chess Championships

I must remember I am not Botvinnik.
And this is home, somewhere to *relax*,

somewhere where she dreams I'm being bedsocks
and she herself is nothing but her toes.

Water for My Mother

To my mother, like a frail pot-plant
that nobody knows how to care for,

all I have to offer is some water
and withering glances of contempt.

My Mother and Men

My mother doesn't like the kind of men
who march about the kitchen cracking jokes;

she only likes the kind who sit in corners
and know what's what. Like succulents, or clothes brushes.

My Mother's Elegance

Yes, my mother's elegant, we know that –
a million times more elegant than I am –

but also slightly bowed, as if by sacs
in which she stores what must remain unsaid.

My Mother's Doctor

I mustn't stroke, or even touch, the cardigan
he mustn't turn and drop into the grass,

he mustn't ask me why I don't stop laughing
and why my tears roll down my cheeks like rain,

I mustn't stop or even think of stopping
although the sun is blinding me like Klimts

and plating me, or coating me, with gold;
I mustn't laugh so much I can't think.

My Mother at Night

If she were a pig she would be grunting –
because she is already half-asleep,

disintegrating, almost, like a pig
surrendering herself to being crackling,

crackling or scratchings; like a pig
that grunts so much she doesn't feel a thing.

My Mother in the Bath

Every day she's been getting bonier
and now, today, I find her, in her underwear

stranded on the bottom of the bath
like that thing she dries her stockings on.

My Mother in Heaven

Heaven, if there is such a place,
is occupied by very small ponies,

even-tempered men in white trousers
and my mother, in a rowing-boat,

eating bread and jam with Mr Pickford
and grinning like a stolen chandelier.

FISHTANK

For E.

...who asked me if I would be happy to answer
some questions about my brother and all
I could think about at first were the eggs,
marked HB in pencil on the shell,
and not about my brother at all.

My Brother and the Chocolates

I can see him opening the box
I like to keep my eyes on from my hiding-place

behind the sofa where I hatch my plots.
I can see an elbow and a leg.

My Brother's Pipe

Brothers neither drive nor smoke which means
this man who drives and smokes is someone else.

My Brother at Night

To him who drives a Riley up a mountainside –
like somebody who dances the tango

without a partner far into the night –
normal rules no longer apply.

My Brother's Shoulders

I sit here for a very long time.
Suddenly my brother reappears,

puts me on his shoulders and strides off.
I'm not as happy as I ought to be

because he keeps on begging me (with threats)
not to keep on stroking his eyelids.

My Brother's Fish

Everybody calls him a doctor
but I myself know better: a doctor

needs to have a stethoscope. And fish.
He does however smell like a doctor.

My Brother and Santa Claus

When I scream at him to go away
he whips his beard off. And I scream some more.

I don't know who is who or who I hate
or how to exorcise that lumpy sack.

My Brother's Party

Teams are picked, sofas rearranged
and people wander round in funny hats

then someone lays me down on an eiderdown
bespangled with a hundred tiny clementines.

My Brother's Shoes

Men who wear suede shoes are all *cads*
so when my brother creeps into the kitchen

wearing what appear to be suede shoes
I naturally conclude he's not my brother.

My Brother's Tie

He always wears a scrappy little tie
I've only ever seen him take off

on summer days when it's been so hot
the only thing to do is go swimming.

My Brother's Hands

The way my brother rubs his hands together,
those big dry hands, makes me back away

and wriggle to my place behind the sofa
where everything revolves around *me*.

My Brother in Tennis Shorts

He's found a ball and some enormous shorts
and yellow sandshoes tied with yellow string.

His hair is thick and rigid like a privet hedge.
His unforced errors make my heart sink.

My Brother as a Maybug

Like somebody disguised as a maybug –
those crackly things that crash against our windows
on summer nights – he is often seen

striding through the fields in an oilskin
that nearly comes down to his ankles.

My Brother's Patients

I never hear a word about the patients
whose groans of pain I like to imagine

echoing along the halls of palaces
that smell of iodine and captive cheetahs.

My Brother's Papers

At night my brother like a giant ram
sits alone in the wingback chair

writing notes that no one else can read
on sheets of paper with the wrong address.

My Brother's Mother

She loves the way he tells her what to do,
and trembles with obedience and relief

to hear the rules again which however
I understood do not apply to him.

My Brother's Bacon

He needs to eat his bacon *in peace*
and not to be sneered at as he does so

by someone who eats nothing but tomatoes
and isn't even clean or fully dressed.

My Brother's Door

He's like a creature that's so rarely seen
it isn't so much seen as imagined.

It lives alone, deep in a forest,
silent but for little grunting noises.

My Brother's Voice

Because my bed is next to the music room
I lie awake and listen to him practising

and every now and then I hear him stop
and whisper *sorry sorry* to no one.

My Brother's Eggs

My brother, stocked with hard-boiled eggs
and bars of chocolate, will be gone all day.

Twice a year he goes with his mother
(without the eggs, as far as the letter-box).

My Brother's Jolly Side

My brother's got a suspect jolly side
that, like the life-sized poster at the station

advertising *teeth-whitening products*,
I can't help feeling fond of him for.

My Brother's Questions

He takes me in a taxi to a restaurant,
sits me down and asks me lots of questions,

none of which I answer, then I leave,
my sequinned handbag catching on my mini-skirt.

I walk into the middle of nowhere,
watching men and women turn to dust.

My Brother on the Lawn

He comes and stands beside her on the lawn
like someone by a pond who watches carp;

who feels, in his quiet way, the feelings
the carp themselves are too ashamed to feel.

My Brother's Flute

I do not like it when he plays the flute
because he is transformed: he leaves behind

the man he was and becomes a man
who seems to want to break his own heart.

My Brother's Chair

He spends his evenings in a dusty chair
like a rare but well-mannered animal

wheedled from its crate and given sherry
to help him not remember his true home.

My Brother on My Wedding Day

The day my brother 'gives me away'
to some strange man he's never seen before

who might as well have been a *loft conversion*,
I take no notice of him whatsoever.

My Brother's Eyes

Because my brother's eyes are like diamonds
still aching from the chill of the mines,

I look not at his face but at the cufflinks
that have no eyes for me to fail to meet.

My Brother's Nose

My brother's got an enviable house,
a secretary, a chauffeur – and a nose

that everybody secretly agrees
in a perfect world would be less long.

My Brother's Spectacles

On summer afternoons he can be found
reading from an ancient book – or staring at it,

like a large and flightless bird in spectacles
that's spent a million years in captivity.

My Brother's Heart

As the winter snow falls thick and fast
my brother's heart inside his jacket beats

hot and tiny like the universe
when, or if, the universe began.

At Home with My Brother

He seems to be uneasy about something
but what that something is we'll never know.

All we know for certain is the chocolate
and days when only chocolate makes sense.

LAMBCHOP

An Elderly Silver-haired Gentleman

An elderly silver-haired gentleman
disappears into a tall house

in which a girl is standing on a sofa
swinging a marmalade cat.

The Tulips

As he takes his vase of mauve tulips
across the hall, he catches sight of her

running up the stairs in her uniform.
He glimpses her unbearable face.

The Tennis Players

They file past and never even notice
the girl in yellow shorts and yellow sandals

balancing on top of the wall
wondering why they look in pain.

The Chandelier

Because a chandelier has got no face
a chandelier can't talk or even smile.

What it does is take its time. The man,
also, looking down, takes his time.

The Swan

The elderly silver-haired gentleman
is like a swan, irascible and bored –

bored by others, not by himself
for whom he works daily in his studio.

The Walking-stick

As if to say why talk when you can stare
(and even the way he stares at her is polished)

he leans against his polished walking-stick
and stares at her until she runs away.

The Taxi

How odd to think the little girl is me
watching from my window as my father

emerges like a goddess from a taxi
brandishing a jubilant bouquet.

The Telephone

The telephone is kept in the cloakroom
and only used for ordering his taxis

and sometimes to invite himself to tea
with those who are too timid to refuse him.

The Man Next Door

Everyone's too old to look after me
but I can look after myself.

The only problem is the man next door
who tells me to *go home and eat soap.*

The Pigeons

The stairs are very steep and the carpet
is slippery, especially in the dark

when everything is in a different place
from where it is or should be in the daytime

and sometimes I can hear funny noises
behind the doors. It's only the pigeons.

The Forest

The man is like a man in a forest
and if he sees me nobody must know.

Girls

Anguillophiles lure their eels with minnows,
the shepherdess her tiny gods with sheep

but gods and eels slip away like water:
girls, however, can be firmly grasped.

The Window

I take the little stone from my pocket
and hurl it at the window then run back

past the entrance to the studio
and up three flights of stairs to my room

from which the sound of pigeons can be heard
who sound as if they gargle with marimba balls.

The Perfume of His Fabulous Pomade

The perfume of his fabulous pomade
billows round me like a sheet or shawl

to settle on my face like a ghost
that's desperate to kiss me but it can't.

The Jack Russell Terrier

I never stop vibrating, like a wasp,
or like a little Jack on a shoot:

I'm wily, cute and godless – and I'm not,
as everyone agrees, to be trusted.

The Doctors

At last they have arrived. Throughout the house
everyone is talking in whispers.

They're saying that the innards of his innards
will now be held in place by a truss.

The Fly

On the polished table in the dining-room
somebody has placed a warm plate

over which a little fly is hovering,
attracted by the succulent chop.

Cutlery

Now that I've been moved to the attic
tiptoeing downstairs takes much longer:

I wait until he's safely in the dining-room
polishing the cutlery with vests.

The Bandages

I'm lying on my back and the hands
of someone I'm imagining adoring me

are binding me and binding me with bandages
smelling of the pink and yellow wafers

and wafers in the shape of ladies' fans
I steal from the tins of children's kitchens.

The Kitten

It's so high up up here that noone knows
if someone keeps a kitten in a shoebag,

least of all the pigeons on the window-ledge
who close their eyes and mind their own business.

The Hornet

The hornet is the size of a mouse.
The tennis-players never stop playing.

Underneath my vest a sickly ladybird
mistakes my hairless armpit for a velodrome.

The Restaurant

I'm walking round the tables to the Ladies
when suddenly I simply walk out –

I walk and walk and never look back
to where the white-haired gentleman sits waiting

behind his dainty table-for-two.

The Nurse

The nurse's hair's tied back like golden syrup
if syrup can be said to be tied back;

the old man's hair is silver, like an ice-pack,
or Jackson Pollock, fractious in L.A.

The Patient

The doctor has instructed his patient
to wear it for the rest of his life.

I rarely see him now, he lives apart,
sheathed in silks and satins like a bey.

The Lily

I never liked him. Creepy as a lily.
A lily made of ice made of icing sugar.

Because He Never Sleeps

Because he never sleeps I want to strangle him
and lay him out out cold on his bed

where he can lie and contemplate for ever
his silver curls and his golden shoes.

His Hairy Ears

Although he's now too old to protest,
his hairy ears still quiver like the ears

of Antonio Stradivari of Cremona
on hearing me tiptoe past his door.

The Lamb

He thought I was his lamb and he could slaughter me
but he was wrong. He should have known. Alas,

I ran away; I ran like the wind;
I ran for fifty years without stopping.

The Pear

The gentleman is weak. He can no longer
do the things he used to do. All day

he lies in bed as in a warm tureen,
as sleepy as a stew or a pear.

Visitors

The elderly gentleman dislikes
visitors, I'm sorry to say,

particularly women who are kind.
And when I say dislikes I mean *despises*.

The Bucket

He had no friends, he had outlived them all,
the funeral passes almost unnoticed

like someone brushing quail off a plate
after midnight into a bucket.

The River

I didn't even go to the funeral.
What's the point? I went to the river

to watch the swans whose quadruplets' serenity
may or may not simply be indifference.

The Cow

I talk as if I'm talking in my sleep,
and even how I walk is like a cow,

I walk as if I'm seeing if it's possible
to walk in time to how my lashes bat.

Suddenly One Morning

Suddenly one morning I wake up
to find that I can do it so I do it.

The only thing that's present is the present.
The past can now do nothing else but shrink.

The Tall House

Now other people live in the house,
other people turn the silver key,

other people chase the lazy pigeons
down the garden with their new brooms.

THE BOXER KLITSCHKO

The Little Pond

The little pond is a perfect fit.
When I take my clothes off and lie down

it feels like I'm lying down in bed,
the water like a sheet I'll never touch

from which freshwater shrimp are peeping out
as if at the arrival of a goddess.

The Picnic

Everyone is sitting by the river
looking very bored on their picnic rugs

and I am on a rock below the waterfall.
My mother says I mustn't show off.

My Cow and Fish Dream

My bed and all my things are underwater
and outside in the garden two big cows

are floating through the roses like two fish
as if to say *why walk when you can swim.*

The House-mistress's Chow

The ornamental pond in the grounds,
instead of fish, contains tiny girls

terrified of meeting the Chow
that likes to eat the tiny girls for dinner.

The Elephant House

When the lifeguard with his yellow hair
keeps falling off his stool and the water

doesn't look like water, I decide
to make myself an elephant house instead.

My Grandfather's Biscuit

On Saturdays he teaches me to swim.
He tells me what to do and I do it.

His butler waits outside in the car
and, as they leave, he passes me a biscuit.

When My Diamond-studded Sisters Scream

When my diamond-studded sisters scream
I crawl into the river on all fours

and wrap myself in mud like a hippo
dreaming of a home in Gondwana Land.

My Hamster, Concrete

Because the pool is my idea of Heaven –
the women in their world of wire baskets,

the concrete underfoot and the dandelions –
I call my concrete-coloured hamster Concrete.

Jelly Beans

Like the monolithic hippopotamus
who spends her days half-submerged in mud

crunching lily roots, I spend my days
beside, or in, the river, sucking jelly beans.

What I Saw in the Changing-Rooms

I can't make out a single word they say.
All I do is stare in disbelief.

(I never tell my mother what I saw:
I wasn't meant to be there in the first place.)

Why They Wear Bikinis

Up and down I go like the others –
but the others know what they are doing

and who they are and why they wear bikinis.
I myself have never worn bikinis.

The Waterfall

It takes me half a day to stumble home –
half a day trying not to whimper.

The water is so cold it's like a Bulldog clip,
or several Bulldog clips, on stiffened nipples.

On Holiday with My Mother and Two Sisters

Why are we here in a guest-house full of canaries
with nothing to see except the Atlantic Ocean

from which I have emerged too stiff with cold
to take the ginger biscuit someone offers me?

The Regulars

They squeeze together on the wooden benches,
completely naked, talking non-stop.

Perhaps they are inventing their own language.
Perhaps they are too naked to be sane.

Goose

She stuffs me till I gag like a goose
and like a goose I can hardly waddle

until the day I learn to disobey –
and once you disobey you can't stop!

What My Mother Says and What She Does

It makes no difference what she says or does,
I want to not be seen and not be handled;

I want to disappear underwater
like a prayer prayed by an eel.

The Weekend at the Lake

Yes, my mother and her friends were right –
I was being watched, and then touched.

I still remember trembling all over
and trying to run away and not being able to.

Stranger

I am now a stranger who my mother
finds herself terrified of,

an incoherent, weather-beaten stranger
she doesn't understand how to please.

Underwater

I introduce my body to the fish
who no one's told I don't know who I am;

how, outside, in the air, I've got a face
I struggle to arrange and rearrange.

The Egg

In a chest of drawers in the drawing-room
I come across a giant chocolate egg

that somebody had given someone else
years ago when everyone was happy.

Matron

I'd run away from school once before
and now the matron goes completely nuts.

The water is pitch black and full of weed.
And she – the matron – can't even swim.

The Pool in Winter

In my so-called 'racing-back' swimsuit,
I slither down inside the heated water

while outside in the snow normal people
go about their business in thick coats.

Selflessly Making Me Hot Meals

The person in the pool with tiny ears,
a piglet's elegant ankles and a body

as muscle-bound and glittering as Klitschko's,
counting while she holds her breath, is me.

People say my mother is a saint
spending all her time in the kitchen

selflessly making me hot meals.
Other people say she spends her days

lounging on the sofa and ignoring me.
Actually, she's *suffocating* me.

My Mother's Ironing-board

I walk about the house like a king –
my matted hair, my gold and silver clothes,

the king-like way I ridicule her ironing-board –
and as I walk I creak my fancy boots.

The Man I Didn't Know

While he wanders off to look for coffee
I wade still fully dressed into the sea.

(I was like that then. I'd do anything
not to talk to men I didn't know.)

Eating Cake outside Europe's Biggest Swimming-pool

Europe's biggest swimming-pool is empty
except for one very small man

whose butler is outside in the carpark
listening to the news and eating cake.

Girls Who Disobey

Girls who disobey are like kings.
I can do anything I want

and everywhere I go I hear the squeak
of men and women fleeing with their wheelbarrows.

Meeting My Uncle for the First Time

So there he is, waving, on the platform –
a man who likes to spend his days at sea,
his evenings at the pub with his Newfoundlands –

and what I do or don't do, he is telling me,
is *up to me*. He doesn't know or care
that I am what my mother calls 'unmanageable'.

My Uncle's Blanket

At first I am a little bit afraid –
the smell of meat, the stiff electric blanket –

but how can I be frightened in a house
where every window overlooks the sea?

Breakfast at My Uncle's

The bread is white and soft and the jam
is ruby-red and the butter-knife

balanced on the butter-dish is silver.
The silver blade is shaped like a rudder.

Everything is friendly-looking. Greenfly
befriend each other on the cabbage roses.

Everywhere You Go There Is Sea

Yes, everywhere you go there is sea
and everyone we meet are his friends –

but I'm not really used to having friends.
I'm not really used to singing neighbours,

'elevenses', polygamy, camellias,
Alka-Seltzer, oystercatchers, oyster beds,

rattling palms and aftershave lotion;
the fact my uncle is 'a naval man';

the pub, the booming voices and the door
where someone will appear with the crisps

I eat with lemonade and later shandy
sitting on the wall in the sun

where everything is now completely different
and everywhere you look there are boats.

A Love of Horses

Everyone prefers boats to horses
except for one malodorous aunt

who wears enormous boots and a stock.
Her eyelids are the colours of macaws.

Magnetism

She's asking me to get the special knife
that lives above the fridge on a magnet

but even just approaching it unnerves me
which spoils the enjoyment of the cake.

My Uncle in the Shower

My uncle is as tall as a mast,
his voice is like a voice made of thunder.

I hear him in the shower every morning
and wonder how the mermaids make love.

My Uncle's Kippers

The bubbliest and sweetest of the aunts
is pouring maple syrup onto waffles

when in he comes, slaps me on the back
and readjusts the knobs on the radio.

The smell of kippers mingles with the smell
of something she has squirted on her hair.

My Uncle's Bread-slicer

I could watch it slicing bread all day!
It's powder blue – like the Virgin Mary

which is odd because the Virgin Mary
would never stay indoors and slice and slice.

My Uncle's Morris Traveller

Inside the Morris Traveller trays of eggs
are heating up in the midday sun.

Everything is heating up. The bonnet,
like a horse, is attracting flies.

My Uncle's Boathouse

Although I love the boats and the boathouse
I never go to sea with the others

because at sea the sea is much too big
and birds have got no trees in which to warble.

My Uncle's Newfoundlands

When I'm tired of living with my face
and helping it make facial expressions

I take my uncle's dogs to the creeks
to paddle their palmatisected feet.

The Mermaid

Not for me, of course, but for my uncle,
the furious aunts produce elaborate cakes –

a mermaid on a rock, for example,
a cherry cut in half for each breast.

My Uncle's Sunroom

Everywhere you turn there are teddies
that lie around with nothing to do.

The dogs are either swimming or asleep
(and even in their sleep they are swimming).

My Uncle's Sandwiches

Every afternoon he makes me sandwiches
which fall apart and smell of cigarettes

and afterwards we share a Wagon Wheel,
or two, or three, without telling anyone.

The Relationships Between Numbers

My uncle's car is full of bits of string
and oyster-shells and lumps of serpentine

which roll around the sandy car like numbers,
with numbers' strange but beautiful relationships.

Heaven

We take a yellow cabbage to the hens
then carry on downhill to the boats,

my uncle in his little crumpled hat,
me in shorts, half-hidden in the hair

my lipsticked aunts, well-meaning as they are,
will later rub in vain with heated groundnut oil.

They never even say what groundnuts are!
All they ever say is how *uncouth* I am;

how I just arrived one summer's day –
'intoxicated by my mother's martyrdom' –

to find the biggest house I could imagine,
inhabited by no one but an uncle

who grinned from ear to ear, his fluffed-up Newfoundlands
greeting me by stealing all my cake

as if to say *we're not big dogs for nothing!*
The aunts are housed in prefabs in the grounds.

One of them secretes in her handbag
supplies of purple raspberry-flavoured cough-syrup.

Another one has wandered off to Africa
where soon she'll die, of what he calls *bewilderment.*

So here I am, ascended into Heaven,
but at the aunts', if not the dogs', expense.

Shoes

From my bedroom I can hear the crunch
of large and small and medium-sized shoes –

the postman's, the milkman's, the beautician's;
and those, if you can call them shoes, of aunts.

The Shop

In the garden wall I find a door
that takes me to a lane and a shop

where every day I buy myself some Spangles
and eat them one by one on the boat.

The Smallest of the Aunts

Although she is the smallest of the aunts
she wears the biggest glasses, which are red,

and round her neck she ties a red bandanna –
or not exactly 'ties' but somehow twists it

in and out of rings made of snakes.
She stands beside the kettle eating nougat

in figure-hugging slacks. With scarlet nails
she peels back the paper you can eat.

119

Walking to the Boathouse

The boathouse is so far from the path
I walk for what seems hours before I reach it

and never meet a soul unless you count
a heron or an egret as a soul.

The Tiny Sunhat

The tiny sunhat, whiter than a pearl,
that one of his many lipstick-encrusted wives

forced on him, I can just imagine it,
the hat on which the sun is always shining

and under which he's balanced on a ladder
painting and repainting his *Celeste*,

the hat is much too small for the head
glinting in the sun as if to prove

the only thing worth living for is baldness –
and having me to visit him and polish it.

If I Want To Be a Hippopotamus

If I want to be a hippopotamus,
or pretend to be one, then I can –
a hippo who can laugh
and make a honking noise,
whose skin's so tough it makes exceptional whips;

whose mouth is like an adolescent piano;
who chews the roots of lilies with her lips;
a hippo who can see underwater
and hold her breath for as long as thirty minutes;
who likes to bounce along the sandy river-bed

and irritate the grumpy crocodiles;
a hippo who is home to little fish;
a hippo God forgot to teach to swim;
who's saying *not to worry*; and who's thanking Him
for giving her her waterproof ears.

The Yacht

One afternoon we make a chocolate yacht
in which he says he thinks he hears my mother

singing songs about a chocolate baby
he says she's having fun feeding jelly.

Take the Little Boat

Take the little boat and your swimming things
and glide without a sound between the trees

and tie the little boat to a root
and dive into the dark like a rat.

What My Mother Wanted

It felt so good to be so disobedient,
to take no notice of my frantic mother

who wanted me to give her what she wanted
but neither of us knew what that was;

it felt so sweet to be so uncontrollable
and not to know what happens to the wronged.

HELPLESS WITH LAUGHTER

Ankles

Everyone looks prettier when they smile
but even when I'm smiling my ankles
need to look practically transparent

and not unlike the eight spindly ankles
of Isak Dinesen's deerhounds, Dawn and Dusk.
Otherwise even then I won't be.

Arm

He rode a pony, bareback, with one arm,
and I was perched in front, on his jacket,
and in this way we left my father's grounds
and rode together down the long road

to find his arm, he said; but now I knew
the man was on his way to find the island
where no one is allowed to set foot
except for those like him without one arm.

Armpits

I shaved my armpits several times a day
and moved around as slowly as I could

and never got upset about a thing
because I was so terrified of sweating.

I sat behind my desk like a morgue
reassembled as a teenager.

Belly

I never saw, far less touched, her belly –
or what she called, or would have called, her stomach –

that must have been as silky as the belly
of Agatha Christie's Manchester Terrier, Treacle.

Biceps

My biceps are as tiny as two mice
that live inside my sleeves and think they're rats.

Body

Is my body me? And – or *or* –
I've also heard a rumour it's a *temple*!

But if it really is, my question is
what do I go in there to bow down to?

Does being kind always lead to happiness?
Is being kind in fact the *only* way?

But what about the swimming-pool attendant?
He makes me happy not because he's kind –

he hasn't even noticed I exist! –
he makes me happy for the simple reason

he and I both like swimming,
preferably naked in my case.

Body Parts

When I'm sad I visualise my body parts
resting in a Garden of Rest,

or some of them in buckets, but all dead,
and being dead, incapable of longing.

Blood

I either call him Slimeball or Scumbag.
(A slimeball is the same as a scumbag.)

It only has to be a tiny touch,
like mist against my skin, and I panic.

My skin is like the Garden of Eden,
by which I mean *supersensitive*.

When we die at death our sense of touch
is thought to be the last to fade away.

My grandmother called the speck of blood
inside the quails' eggs a *fleck* of blood.

We can call it what we like, she said,
but every child has to eat her egg.

I may be stupid but I'm not that stupid.
Blood that's in the egg is still blood.

Bone

Marvel at the bone inside my skin,
ingenious and vigilant, like joy,

that once belonged to someone called my mother,
dressed in pink and blue and bored to tears.

Bottoms

Cushions are like pups for bony bottoms:
they may be cuddly but they've no idea

which way up they're meant to be or where,
or what they're meant to not be not be doing.

We have to plump them up like the hairdos
of women in despair on promenade.

Brain

The toes I used to use to paint the toenails of
I'm using now in what was then the future

to cheer me up by wiggling in warm sand
while in my head my patient brain is resting.

Breastbone

Do you know why breastbones are more flexible
in women than in men? And also where

the limits of, or to, compassion lie?
Of my compassion in particular?

Breasts

Although my breasts behave like no one loves them
I buy them bras like jellyfish to humour them,

brightly coloured ones with lots of stretch
or not so brightly-coloured but more frilly ones.

Calves

By 'snow-white calves' I mean my snow-white legs
and not my little snow-white cows, unfortunately.

Cheeks

His soups, his clocks, his mussel-coloured cheeks,
his floor-length gown, the way he used to tremble

I knew every detail but was spared
 his private thoughts as he was spared mine.

Chin

I see it's not a problem for my grandson –
who may or may not have a chin like Clint,

whose chin is lost in rolls of fat like sleeping-bags
but must be somewhere – not to be like him.

Collarbone

Please can I have a bony collarbone;
also a love of earwigs and the elderly.

Please can I have an entymologist,
preferably a swimming entymologist.

And please can I have a little long-legged wolfhound pup
capable of flooring a grown man.

Please can I have an effective anti-perspirant,
some oxytocin nasal spray,
a toothmug,
a colouring-in book
Reese's,
effortless chic,
including what the finishing schools called salt cellars.
And please can I have slim knees like dead storks.

And also the Qu'ran in twenty languages.
And, most of all, a photo of The King.
Not just any photo. One with Gladys.

Don't forget – it must be one with Gladys.

Crotch

They say it in a lower tone of voice,
Very slightly lower but still lower.

And not just little men in raincoats either.
Also larger men not in raincoats.

Cuticles

I need to be aware of my cuticles
that need to be as perfect as the cuticles –

or anyhow that's the way I picture them –
the cuticles of Elvis Presley's mother,

including those mysterious half-moons.
I hope you know exactly what 'half-moons' are.

Ears

I only see the birds and not the ears
whose tiny holes I keep as clean as whistles.

Elbows

A cricket is a kind of violinist
that plays not violins but itself.

I used to think they played with their elbows
but now I know it's actually their wing-cases.

Eye

Even my own mother has been seen
charging at full speed down the lawn.

(Afterwards she'll look a bit sheepish,
her tennis shoes, or 'sand-shoes', streaked with green.)

And if they *keep their eye on the ball*
even girls are allowed to play.

Eyelashes

The eyelashes of ostriches and camels
are very thick and make them look like film stars.

Mine are thin.
And I don't spit.

Eyelids

Owls and sloths have special sideways eyelids
but even mine though mine are miraculous:

they work away all day and all they get
is slices of cold cucumber and kohl.

Face

My rosy face still can't believe it tolerated
all those kisses we mistook for love

because we were afraid and turned away
towards what we were even more afraid of.

Feet

After school I climb onto the wall
and sit and watch the tennis players. Often

bits of red brick wall become dislodged,
sometimes with a puff of red brickdust.

Finger

As if it has forgotten it's an axe,
the axe is on the floor, and my finger,

as if it's not a finger but a feather,
is fingering the edge of the blade.

Fingernails

I was small and on the verge of tears
but had she somehow stopped herself and visualised
Federer's distinctive, lofty back lift

nothing like what happened would have happened
and she would have embraced with open arms
even those with dirty toe- and finger-nails.

Fringe

Can't they understand my fringe is private
and no one is allowed to even think about it

any more than they're allowed to think about
the private thoughts of the one-armed groom?

Groin

Is a groin the same as a lap?
A *groin* is like the word for an animal
that's very large, with very small eyes,

and so it seems a shame if it's a lap
and anyway a lap is not a thing
because it isn't there when it's not.

Hair

Hair must be *dead straight*, like my mother's,
that looks as if a spider has spun it,

its little face frowning from its dell
as if there is a law against the curly kind.

Hands

At the age of four I saw Jesus
hanging on His cross by His hands

but I was only four and didn't know
a word must have a meaning – for example,

unresolved. It means unresolved.
And *longing* means, as we know, longing.

Head

Like rising dough that's terrified of draughts,
I'm hiding in my grandmother's airing-cupboard

pretending to myself I've got no head
while savouring the heat's uneventfulness.

Hearts

They're tiptoeing towards me in the dark –
but when I say 'towards me' do the spiders

know I'm here or am I, like a god,
too big for them to know? – they tiptoe round

as if to say why sleep when you can tiptoe,
although their hearts must be extremely small.

Heels

I will not let the fact that they look like cabbage stalks
perturb the imperturbable composure

it's taken me sixty years to cultivate –
sixty years to reinvent the cabbage!

Hymen

You think it sits there in my mind's eye
perfectly correct in every detail –

size and small, colouring, consistency
and nothing like a hymnal – but it doesn't.

Iris

The iris and the palate and the hip
seem to want to say they *like it here*,

inside my body, like the woolly mould
inside the petri dish the mould calls home.

Jaw

I've never seen my jaw but I've felt it:
it feels like a jaw made of roses

and I don't mind a bit if at times
peagreen aphids wander by and tickle it.

Kidney

Is God paying attention? When I die
please can I be useful to somebody?

Somebody who'd rather be alive.
And please can they not subsequently murder someone.

Knees

I prayed to God for knees like a camel
but now He is insisting I have knees

that might as well be turnips they've so fat
so yes, He knows a camel's knees go backwards

but no, I must accept *I'm not a camel.*
Otherwise I will offend my knees.

Lanugo

Anorexics, foetuses and cancer patients
grow lanugo on themselves that glimmers

gold against their silver limbs like pampas grass
whose gold can be so pink it looks creamy.

Lips

The bone-dry grasses irritate my face
as if I'm in their way, as if their lips

can barely speak they hate me so much;
as if they'd rather die than be greasy.

Lungs

I know you don't believe me but my lungs
still remember the enormous weight

that pressed them down until they gave up hope
like froglets in some decommissioned reservoir.

Muscles

Applying embrocation to my muscles,
I hear, or think I hear, a distant chink,

like sherbet lemons in a plastic cup,
but by the time I realise what it is,

or what it was, or might have been, it's gone;
so why would I have thought it could have been

happiness? (Either sherbet lemons,
lemon sherbets, either way is fine.)

Navel

Thankful for small mercies as I am,
such as that I'm not afraid of wasps,

I'm thankful for the navel which a stranger
knotted for me late one autumn night

outside an upstairs room in which my mother
was praying I was just a bad dream.

Neck

If I were a head on a cushion
even if I wouldn't still be me

at least I wouldn't have to have a neck
for him to criticise and me to scrub.

Nerves

Never underestimate my mother
and never underestimate the shock –

especially when her nerves are so bad
the slightest think reduces her to tears –

of witnessing the *goal celebrations*
she celebrates on tiptoe in a onesie.

Nipples

Nobody, least of all the dog,
an overweight bull terrier called Rosemary
who liked to pin small children to the floor,

nobody, in those days, could be trusted,
but all the same I let her share my bed
(with both her dried up nipples) where she died.

Nose

I'm not exactly saying that I *like* it
but I do *feel for* the nose

that's longing to take refuge once again
inside the relative darkness of the Wombat House.

Nostrils

Surrounding me like God in all directions,
and fiddling with my nostrils, is my absence –

an absence that's so vast it fills the universe
and everything that's in it, except me.

Penis

Enthusiastic men and women everywhere
are having sex regardless of the word

but for me the little word *penis*
puts me off although I know it shouldn't.

Ribcage

The nuns who dug their thumbs into my ribcage
may or may not now be in Heaven.

Saliva

Although my father's coats were full of sweets,
and every night I'd watch him spread them out

and pick the most attractive ones and suck them,
he never gave any to me.

Shoulder-blades

They're big and white and shaped like the wafers
gods might order with their Poire Hélène.

Two of them. Like constricted fins.
I've never seen them but I know they're there

and probably, to answer your question,
I think they are the part I like the best.

Shin

It's like when you're alone with the bereaved,
saying *shin* makes me slightly nervous,

so what I'll do is say the word *shin-pad*
over and over again until I'm used to it.

Skull

My skull is like an overhead locker
full of stuff no one's going to need.

Forgiveness? I don't know. Put it this way,
I think I've come to terms with who he is.

Soul

Polishing a hen, say, or tomatoes,
I can understand, but a lake?
How can someone *polish a lake?*

And even if I do possess a soul
and even if my soul is like a lake
and even if I were to somehow polish it

what is it exactly, if anything,
my soul can be expected to reflect?
Is there something I'm not being told?

Spine

As a child I would get enraged
by the stupid way she couldn't walk

but now I am an adult I can see
that's the way the cookie crumbles sometimes.

Teeth

They work at night and live with their mothers
and can't remember living with their fathers

and none of them have touched a naked breast
and none of them can sleep without a light.

and all of them call themselves *killers*
and peel their satsumas with their teeth.

Thighs

Being neither partridges nor sportsmen,
women must *never* have plump thighs.

Throat

Without the hat she would have looked more normal
but even then, without the hat, my mother
would still have somehow *ruined my day*

and what I could not say and never said
would still have spiralled out of sight like larks,
reaching unimaginable heights.

Thumbs

Everything is better in the dark,
his veins against my thumbs, for example.

Toes

The Taj Mahal, like the ancient socks
I wear at night as mother for the toes

freezing at the end of my sleeping-bag,
looks as if it's had it up to here.

Tongue

The sickly colours of my sticks of rock
taste of fish mixed with fishy sugar

in spite of which I sit in bed and lick them
until I feel my tongue growing tails.

Veins

Something I can't name but may be me
races up and down inside my veins

like Arctic hares that race across the Arctic
to prove to snow the benefits of paws.

Vocal Cords

The most important thing about my vocal cords
is not to let them veer towards the subjects

they're not supposed to veer towards like jets
bored by their inflexible trajectories.

Womb

First I'm told the *dates* must be regular,
then I'm told that *I* must be regular.

Regular, regular, regular.
My womb is like a pouch made of trout.

Wrists

They may well be convenient for slashing
but wrists are here to keep your bracelets warm

and stop your hands from falling off and anyway
slashing them doesn't even work.

Wristbone

Only my wristbone is thin.
It's like an earwig who is so bored
she falls asleep on her wedding-day!

(and, by the way, about the photograph,
don't forget: it must be one with Gladys.
Gladys looks so pretty when she smiles.)